A LOVE AFFAIR

with God

Dr. Patricia J. Vanderpool

ISBN 978-1-0980-8243-7 (paperback)
ISBN 978-1-0980-8244-4 (digital)

Christian Faith Publishing, Inc.
832 Park Avenue
Meadville, PA 16335
www.christianfaithpublishing.com

Printed in the United States of America

A FATHER

A father loves wholly, gives silently, teaches softly, and inspires profoundly. A father teaches his children to be thankful so they can be happy. A father teaches life as a miracle. A father provides laughter, inspires dreams, promotes honesty, and demonstrates kindness. A father practices and shows peace. A father displays participation, caring, help, forgiveness, fairness, belief, faith, and action.

What a blessing to have both an earthly father and a heavenly father.

CONTENTS

PROLOGUE

This book is meant to be a friend, a comfort, and a blessing for me, the author, and for you, the reader. This book is meant to enlighten and uplift those seeking a life that involves Jesus Christ, God the Father. It is written in a way that allows for and helps promote a life of faith. The contents and language are selected to easily introduce, support, and educate yourself, your family, and your children of God the Father and His never-ending love for us all. *A Love Affair with God* is spoken in common language that is easily understandable so all ages and levels of intellect can easily enjoy and appreciate what the Lord has to offer.

You will find multiple original prayers for you, the reader, from me, the writer, to use during your daily life and situations of worry or stress. Prayers to learn from, build upon, and make your own as you see fit. This book will open your heart, mind, and emotions to God the Father, scripture, and the Holy Bible. You will be able to easily understand how to incorporate and use the Bible in your daily life. Integration of the Bible in problem solving is also discussed. After all, the Bible is written about and for you.

This book will allow you and me to easily introduce not only children but others around us to God the Father and allow them to experience the comfort and joy of Jesus Christ. This book will prove to be an educational tool, a support system, and an outline of prayer. My hope as the author is that this book will support, show, and teach you to speak to your Heavenly Father as if He is your best friend standing right beside you in every situation. Another goal of this book is to provide you with the strength to reach out to God the Father for comfort in a world of turmoil, strife, and loneliness.

You will read the mind of God through scriptures; the current mentality of humanity as it is today and as it was thousands of years ago and find that it is not that different. You will be exposed to the happiness of believers and will be guided to gain this happiness by reaching out to your Heavenly Father.

CHILDREN OF GOD

> Everyone who is a child of God conquers the
> world. And this is the victory that conquers the
> world—our faith.
>
> —1 John 5:4

You get inpatient with your own life, trying to master a habit or control a sin and in your frustration begin to wonder where the power of God is. Be patient. God is using today's difficulties to strengthen you for tomorrow; He has not forgotten you. He is growing you in faith. He is equipping you, strengthening you, and humbling you. The God who makes things grow from the dirt of the earth will help you grow and bear fruit.

Dwell on the fact that God lives within you. God our Heavenly Father resides in and supports each of us. Think about the power that gives your life. The realization that God is dwelling within you may change the places you want to go and the things you want to do today and every day of your life. This Godly presence will cause you to speak kinder, care deeper, and show compassion in situations you would rather not, but your grace is stronger than others negativity and demons.

Do what is right this day and every day, whatever it is, whatever comes down the path, whatever problems and dilemmas you face, just do what's right. Maybe no one else is doing what's right, but you do what's right. You be honest. You take a stand. You be true. After all, regardless of what you do, God does what is right He saves you with his grace.

Each of the Bible verses mentioned comes from the King James Version (KJV) of the Holy Bible.

CHAPTER 1

Protector and Keeper

Our Heavenly Father is wise and divine, His love surrounds us all the time. In daylight, He guides us through right and wrong, leading us forward to where we belong. In the dark of night with stars shining bright, our Heavenly Father is holding us tight. His gentle hand gives a caress and soothes the being we all possess.

Protection and peace, He offers up if we sip from His life flowing cup. The hedge of protection is God's guarantee that nothing will harm either you or me. When speaking to God, we thank Him for this and for all the pleasures He allows to exist. Pray in the morning and again at night, pray that God help you spread His light.

Pray for help and pray for peace alike; nothing is too big or too small for God and His abounding love. God the father desires to be good to you. God wants to see you happy and flourishing as your growth reflects the love of your Heavenly Father. Pray bold prayers and ask for the desires of your heart. Have faith and patience that your prayers are already answered in God's timing.

Pray your prayer and give thanks to God for what He has already done in your life. Talk to God and thank Him for what He will do in your life in the future. Talk to God as if you were speaking to your earthly father. Express your heart, your fear, your excitement, and your sorrow to God the father, for He is and always will be with you. Talk to God when you need a friend, a companion, a mentor, and a guide. God the Father is always and forever by your side. Live your life knowing you are never alone. Live knowing God has prepared for you a heavenly home.

> The Lord is my shepherd I shall not want.
> —Psalm 23:1

My prayer for you:

Heavenly Father, as we come before you again to express our love and ask forgiveness of sin. Thank you, Father, for making me whole, thank you, Father, for dwelling in my soul. It's you I will praise and offer rejoice because you, God, are my only choice. Thank you, Father, I am strong and content. Thank you, Father, my faith is not bent. I share this prayer with all who will read. I share this prayer that we all should succeed. I speak to you freely to help those along that continue to wonder where they belong.

Amen.

CHAPTER 2

Conviction

Children of God seem meek and mild; they do not allow themselves to get riled. Children of God are smart and strong; they understand right and they understand wrong. It's the way that were wired from head to toe; the internal source that helps us grow. Conviction is deep and comes from within, conviction will lead us from beginning to end. Our convictions include our beliefs, principles, morals, and ethics.

Conviction from God is a guiding light. Conviction lets us know if were doing wrong or doing right. Conviction is the feeling that comes from within, the direction we take and each action we make. Your gut feelings and your intuition tend to lean toward your convictions. Trust your convictions and trust God as your conscience comes from the Heavenly Father.

Your Heavenly Father dwells deep within, speaking and leading you clear of all sin. His actions are subtle, His voice is slight, He is our ever-faithful partner in any life fight. When seeking guidance, go with your gut as God the father is backing you up, making you strong, and never going to guide you wrong.

Conviction is that feeling that comes over one when decisions are made, and life comes undone. You know you should act and take a stand; you know you should react and make a mend. That gnawing reaction that comes from within the guidance of God who helps us avoid all sin.

Be patient and listen, don't get in a rush. Ask questions, get answers, plan, and discuss with God your Heavenly Father in whom you trust. If it feels peaceful and easy and progresses as such know it's been blessed by God's affirming touch. If you struggle and fail, fret and worry, step back and look, don't get in a hurry. Maybe God is trying to tell you something, such as you're making the wrong move.

Like your earthly father, the Lord wants you to grow, He wants you to prosper, and good seeds to flow from you and your decision making. He will not stop you from choices you make but will help and guide you with decisions and direction you take.

Be still and listen to God's sacred voice, but remember in the end, it is still your choice. He allows us to fail, be wrong, be sick, be abandoned, and be hurt. But God the Father remains on alert. He will not forsake you for decisions you make. Your Heavenly Father will always be patient as corrections you make, forgiveness you seek, and actions you take.

Conviction is the set of principles we get from the Lord above, the pathway to walk in light and in love.

Be Still and know that I am God.

—Psalm 46.10

My prayer for you:

Heavenly Father, thank you again for the wisdom and guidance you have given us within. We pray to you, Father, for direction and hope, the strength and knowledge and ability to cope. We come to you humbly, our Father, today and praise you for the kindness that you have sent our way. We ask for forgiveness in decisions we make that prove displeasing along the life pathway we take. Oh, Heavenly Father, please lead and direct, make our decisions be filled with your grace; make our decisions be filled with your love; make our decisions something you would be proud of. Continue to lead and guide us we pray; we need your guidance and grace forever, helping us along this earthly life way.

Amen.

CHAPTER 3

The Holy Bible

The Holy Bible is not just a form of history to be discussed it's a representation of us. Topics and stories debated and regurgitated in many forms but not quite as personal as when we read the Bible ourselves and see the life reflections that are uncovered within the stories, verses, and chosen words.

As we read the Bible, we find ourselves immersed in culture, culture of our ancestors, culture of Christ, and culture of the world. Reading the Bible will allow us to see ourselves as God the Father sees us: the true us on the inside. Reading the Bible will allow us to discover where we are falling short in life, ways to improve our lives, and where we are excelling in life as well. Our Bible gives us strength and wisdom in the written word of God the Father.

The Holy Bible is a guide to life well lived. You will find yourself, your soul, and your internal reflection reading the Bible. I encourage you to see the Holy Bible as a restorative to go forward in life and pursue your dreams, seek the desires of your heart, and live the abundant life God wants for all his children.

I also encourage you to see the Holy Bible as a guide to lead and direct your steps in life. Search out scripture written in the Bible to help you deal with particular situations life hands us all, including the death of a loved one, the birth of a child, personal gain, self-help, or any other topic that may interest you or that you may need help in.

Your Holy Bible is a support system in and of itself, all for your use twenty-four hours a day, seven days a week. Your Bible will lead you closer to God. Your Bible will give you strength during trying times when you feel all is lost. Most of all, your Bible is giving you the word of God and the power behind the word of God.

See the Holy Bible as a comfort, the shoulder of God to lean on in times of trouble and trial. The more you search for God in the Bible, the closer to God you will become.

See your Bible as a companion and a friend. A companion and a friend with whom you can discuss anything. Your Bible as part of your daily life and routine is allowing God the Father more time in your life. More time to teach you, more time to praise you, more time to strengthen you.

In our never-ending quest to discover ourselves, the meaning of life, our future, and the past we often forget the most important piece of reference material available to us, the Holy Bible. The written word of God in the Holy Bible will open your eyes and your heart to the world around you as it is, as it once was, and as it could be. We are no different than those in the Bible, we all have troubles and triumphs.

Strive for enlightenment by getting to know yourself with the use of your Bible. God will reveal all you need and want to know if you make the effort to seek out the answers. Don't be stifled by those around you who think negative, criticize your actions, or talk behind your back, they are behind you for a reason!

Search for the Lord in your Bible, you will find Him in His word.

The Bible offers a wealth of wisdom, so read it to be wise. The Bible discusses stories that are as true and relevant today as they were thousands of years ago; read and learn your history. The Bible is a source of strength, support, knowledge, and a resource for happiness, wealth, productivity, and promise.

The Bible is a light at the end of a tunnel we all must walk called death with a promise of life after death. The Bible is a source of comfort for the ailing, downtrodden, downhearted, and frail—use it to cheer yourself and those around you. The Bible will open you to the Lord Jesus Christ and heaven and close the gates of hell as it may be.

An interesting fact: scientists have located a great lake of fire in our solar system, certainly, something to think about and ponder as you make your way through life as a believer in the Heavenly Father. The Bible is a compass to lead and guide you should you desire to use it. The Bible is readily available to anyone willing to open it up and dare peek inside.

> Seek God's will in all that you do, and He will direct your path.
>
> —Proverbs 3:6

My prayer for you:

Lord, thank you for your words. Thank you for this book we call the Holy Bible. Lord, continue to lead, guide, and direct our paths in the ways of your desire. Lord, thank you for the strength, comfort, and wisdom found in the Bible. Heavenly Father, thank you for your kindness and understanding during our times of trial, loneliness, grief, and growth. Again, Lord, thank you for the word of God and the resource you have given us as we strive to lead the best life possible. Lord, thank you for this Holy Bible that serves as a friend and companion in life. Dear Heavenly Father, thank you again for your words in the Holy Bible that serve as a pathway to you and your spirit. Lord, thank you for dwelling in our hearts and our minds. Amen.

CHAPTER 4

Faith

I love the words let your faith be bigger than your fear as fear is the enemy who is repeatedly trying to stifle you, bring you down, steal your joy, and make you believe the worst.

Faith in our Heavenly Father offers hope, supports dreams, and provides us promise of things to come.

The American Heritage dictionary defines faith as a confident belief or trust in a person, idea, or thing that you cannot see, touch, or is not tangible. Faith/Christianity is a secure belief in the existence of God the Heavenly Father and acceptance of His will.

> Faith is the substance of things hoped for, the evidence of things not seen.
> —Hebrews 11:1

Faith allows us to believe in those things yet unseen in our lives. Faith is like the wind, you feel it, can witness its destruction, but you cannot see it. With faith in the Lord, we can believe for healing when the earthly world says there is no hope. Faith allows for hope and weakens the opposition that often is accompanied by anxiety, depression, and generalized loss of well-being.

Faith allows for positive outcomes when you do not see any on your own. We must believe, believe in our Heavenly Father and His divine love for us. We must take positive actions, visualize, and speak to ourselves both inward and outward as we want it to be. Declare by your faith in the Lord Jesus Christ that things are possible even when everything around you tells you they are not.

Having faith that is strong and positive will allow for a foundation in life that will withstand whatever comes your way. Faith in the Heavenly Father will allow you to have a great and prosperous life if you dare to believe it is possible. A life free of fear and death.

For our life is a matter of faith. Not of sight.

—2 Corinthians 5:7

Regardless of your background, faith can allow you to dream anything is possible in your life if you put actions behind it. Your faith must be bigger and stronger than any fear or naysayers that you allow to creep into your thoughts. Your faith must remain strong and steadfast as to avoid the doubts and fears that those around you may project upon you to interrupt your actions.

Keep moving forward in your faith, believing it (the desires of your heart) will happen, and keep striving to make your dreams reality. Beliefs can make a profound difference in failure or success. You must start by believing in yourself as your Heavenly Father believes in you and nothing will seem impossible or out of reach.

As much as we would like to believe they are, everyone is not for you, you will encounter those who wish to see you fail because they cannot succeed themselves. Don't allow yourself to become distracted with the ways of others, maintain your focus and proceed even when you don't see progress. The enemy wants nothing more than to see you get discouraged, fail, lose your faith, and retreat. Always remember worry ends where faith begins.

The Bible discusses a story of a woman whose faith was so strong the mere touch of Jesus robe provided her healing. Matthew 9:22 says, "Your faith in the Heavenly Father has made you whole declares the Lord." Strive for a faith strong enough to receive what your Heavenly Father has in store for you.

The Lord tells us if we have faith, even faith as small as a mustard seed, nothing is impossible for you to accomplish. You must dare to believe it yourself; believe your Heavenly Father is leading your steps and providing for you in every situation. We don't see the wind, but we know it's there as it blows against our skin and we feel it. We watch this invisible force uproot giant trees that have been rooted for thousands of years, destroy miles of property, and cool the hottest summer day. Allow your faith in your Heavenly Father to be as strong as the mightiest storms; uprooting every evil in your life, providing hope when all seems lost, and taking away fears, doubts, and sadness. Our Heavenly Father tells us in Matthew 17:20 that even faith as small as a grain of mustard seed will move mountains if we believe it is possible; it's your decision to believe in the impossible and believe in what you cannot see but hope for.

> Faith does not make things easy it makes them possible.
> —Luke 1:37

This week in history (July 16, 2019), the Apollo 11 mission to the moon took place fifty years ago. There was both a Bible and great faith that accompanied the astronauts to the moon. This is a perfect example of faith and the strong belief that anything is possible if we strive to make it so.

Our faith serves as a vessel to save the soul. Our faith is a gift of God the Father. Faith allows us to believe the promise of life after this earthly experience and death. Faith provides us hope for things unseen and things yet to come. Faith gives us the foundation to seek out the desires of our heart.

We must use our faith to promote our promises, selves, life, and future.

Our faith is a testament to the goodness of God the father and all He has in store for us if we do our part. It is irresponsible to think faith alone will provide you with all you want and need. You must believe in yourself, believe in God the Father, strive daily to reach your goals, work hard, take action, and give thanks to God for all He is allowing you to dream and believe.

Faith provides opportunity if you accept it. Remember, faith without works is dead. Pronounce your faith with your words, your actions, your attitude, and your love. Love for all God's creations, both large and small, quiet and reserved, or known to all; everything under heaven is of the Lord's creation.

The Joy Faith Brings

Faith is to believe what you do not yet see; the reward for this is to see what you believe.

—Saint Augustine

All I have seen teaches me to trust the Creator for all I have not seen.

—Ralph Waldo Emerson

Faith is a sounder guide than reason. Reason can go only so far, but faith has no limits.

—Blaise Pascal

Faith is the function of the heart.

—Mahatma Gandhi

For we walk by faith not by sight.

—2 Corinthians 5:7

Faith is the daring of the soul to go farther than it can see.

—William Newton Clark

Delight yourself in the Lord and He will give you
the desires of your heart.

— Psalm 37:4

My prayer for you:

Lord, thank you for the opportunity that is offered to us by simply having faith in you and faith in your words. Lord, thank you for providing me with everything I need to be successful in my endeavors and in my daily life. Heavenly Father, thank you for once again allowing me to know I have a future, a promise of things to come, and the wisdom to believe in the unseen. Thank you again, Jesus Christ, for placing dreams and desires in my heart and leading me never tiring toward them.

Father, you have promised with faith as small as a seed of mustard, I am destined to an everlasting love and comfort from heaven above. Again, Heavenly Father, thank you for remaining steadfast beside me in my journey along the pathway of life and faith. Amen

CHAPTER 5

Healing

When we talk about healing, we are not only talking about healing the physical wounds of the body. We must also include healing of the mind, soul, and spirit as each of these cause distress in our daily life and disrupt our progress, emotional state, and happiness. In the Bible, Proverbs 3 tells us believing in and maintaining a relationship with Jesus Christ is the healthy option for all human beings. This relationship with the Heavenly Father will promote our well-being. It is thought that individuals with God in their life live approximately 11 percent longer and are happier than nonbelieving persons.

Matthew chapter 8 tells of faith as a means of healing. We must believe and declare our faith in Jesus Christ the Lord that He has and will continue to heal our wounds and our spirits. We must believe fiercely that our bodies can and will be healed of illness and torturing situations. Express your faith in the Lord by stating I am healed, I am well, I am no longer troubled with affliction to my body, my mind, or my soul. The Lord said ask and it shall be given; ask for your healing as in Psalms 6, believe it was done and live. Do your part, treat your affliction with medication as needed, live a healthy lifestyle, eat right, exercise, pray, thank the Lord regularly for His healing hand on your life.

The Lord also expects us to provide healing and comfort to others around us as a testament to our faith. Freely it is given to us so we must freely pass on our faith in the Lord's ability to heal others (Matthew 10:8). Let the faith of healing that comes from the

Heavenly Father show in your words, actions, and promotion of others' healing.

Psalms 30 describes Jesus as our helper and healer. We must cry out to God and ask Him for healing. Rejoice in God and thank Him in advance for the healing of your body, your mind, and/or your spirit. State your healing all throughout the day, proclaim I am healthy, I am healing, I am whole, I am disease free, and never cease. Give praise to God our Heavenly Father who has spared your life and offered the opportunity to live with His word. Praise the Lord that he makes you strong enough to endure your illness and heal.

> So do not fear, I am with you; do not be dismayed, for I am your God. I will strengthen you and help you; I will uphold you with my righteous right hand.
> — Isaiah 41:10

Believe the light of the Lord Jesus Christ is upon you and your life, trust that He will heal you of any affliction threatening your life. Do not give consideration for the illness or despairing thoughts. Do not let doubt cloud your mind or interrupt your spirit. Know that the Lord is in control, is helping you, is healing you. As in Luke 8 and 18, our faith in the Lord will provide us healing when healing in the traditional sense may seem impossible. God says your faith will make you whole.

Matthew 12 tells us to ask God for our healing daily. Seek the goodness of the Lord daily by asking for healing, forgiveness, and mercy and avoid opinions of those who do not have your faith or love for the Lord. Remain ever vigilant in seeking your healing despite those around you and their doubt. Regardless of the situation allow God into your life. Let the Lord Jesus Christ bring light into you that will uplift you and allow you to believe for healing no matter what is going on around you.

Furthermore, do not give merit to the darkness people will try to bring upon you during your trying times. Keep your heart, eyes, and focus upon God and the healing He provides. During times of betrayal as in Luke 22, the Lord remained ever faithful to heal His children.

John chapter 5 tells of healing of those that follow the direction of the Lord and believe He uses angels to help us along life's pathways. Praise the Lord for His healing as in Acts 4. Do not allow others around you to stifle your voice of praise to God for all He has done for you and the healing He provides to you. Praise Him and thank Him for healing you even when you cannot see anything happening. Continue to praise God daily that He is healing you, making you well, and restoring you completely.

Hebrews 12 tells us to be patient and live our life as it was given to us by God. Run our own race and do not allow others to decide our paths. We are all equal; we are all born the same way, and we all must die the same way. Do not allow someone without faith to steal your healing and restoration. Stand strong in your beliefs that God will do as He promised and make you whole.

Your faith in the Lord should bring you comfort knowing He gave his life that you should live and be provided healing.

> Don't worry about anything. Instead, pray about everything. Tell God what you need and thank Him for all He has done.
> —Philippians 4:6

My prayer for you:

Lord, thank you for providing healing when we do not see a way. Thank you for the opportunity to come before you again, knowing we are safe in the arms of God. Thank you for healing our tired and weakened bodies, minds, and spirits. Lord, thank you for allowing us one more day to sing your praises and enjoy everything the world you created has to offer.

Lord, bring healing to those in need. Offer the sick and downhearted your strength and love that they may enjoy the life you have provided and the healing that is within reach if we only believe. Heavenly Father, continue to keep your hedge of protection around us and continue to fill our lives with healing and promise of healing.

Lord, thank you for the hope in my heart and the life in my body. Amen.

On a more personal note: over one year ago, the first week of May around the eighth, ninth, tenth 2019 or so my mother was sent home from one of the best hospitals Indiana has to offer with a death sentence; they gave her no hope and no discussion of healing.

She has an aortic fistula going into her duodenum, essentially a tunnel from the largest blood vessel in the body into her gut causing her to bleed profusely. This fistula cannot be repaired due to her health status. She has had previous repairs for severe vascular disease and a return of cancer to her lung that has metastasized to her brain. This cancer on top of everything else has caused the one surgeon (her age sixty-seven who was disturbed she was rendered helpless as he is sixty-seven and has much life to live and continues to practice) whom was going to try the repair to decide it is no longer an option to repair this tunnel that is going to cause her to bleed to death.

So we came home with the faith in our Heavenly Father that He has His thumb on her aorta and He will maintain her life until He is ready for her to come home—and it is over a year ago and she remains living, not spilling one drop of blood, brain cancer eradicated, lung cancer halted. Healing is yours for the taking, do your part, and ask your Heavenly Father for His help and guidance. Amen.

CHAPTER 6

Love

Love is defined as a deep affection and warm feeling for another as well as a strong fondness and enthusiasm. Every being is capable of feelings of love. Love is witnessed daily all around us in every aspect of our environment.

"We love Him because He first loved us" (John 4:19).

We experience love because the Lord first loved us. John 15:13 states there is no greater love than a man who lay down his life for his friend. The Lord demonstrates His great love for us as He gave His life for His children that they may experience eternal life beyond the grave.

Birth and death are part of the everlasting process of life. In John 3:16, the Lord offers up His son; for God so loved the world that He gave His only begotten son, that whosoever believeth in Him should not perish but have everlasting life. Everlasting life of the spirit and soul, not everlasting life of the body we possess.

The love we enjoy and are capable of allows us to care deeply for another's well-being. This love is first demonstrated by the parental love shown to us by our parents, our grandparents, and our families. The ability to feel strongly toward another, to care about them, show compassion, empathy, and offer affection is the same love afforded by our Heavenly Father, the Lord Jesus Christ.

He is with you from the moment you are born until the moment you die. We call upon the Lord as a friend, as a mentor, as a comfort, a guide, and a source of strength in times of trouble.

We need only ask the Lord into our heart; reach out to your heavenly Father, speak to Him as if you were speaking to your earthly father. Seek comfort in the love of the Lord. He is ever steadfast beside you, dwelling within you in every situation, every location, and every triumph and failure.

Upon asking the Lord into your heart and making Him part of your daily life, you will begin to feel the power and comfort of the Lord. Your focus on Him will calm anxiety and fear. You will never be alone as all you have to do is reach out and speak to the Lord at any time, in any situation, and with faith, knowing He is with you.

It has been statistically proven those who believe in God and have a relationship with Him are happier. Happier with life, happier with themselves, and happier in general. Those who believe in the Lord and have faith are also blessed with a greater life span than those who do not believe or have faith as part of themselves. The love of the Lord allows us to live free from stress, free from strife, and free from worldly ideology and projected negativity. 1 Corinthians 16:14 says, "Let all that you do be done in love."

By following this simple scripture, you are not allowing hatred, fear, intimidation, or deception into your life. Your practice of love in all that you do doesn't allow the negativity of the world around you to decide your fate, your future, or your today. By loving and honoring God as He loves us, we become content, happier, free from condemnation, and free from strife. Love will cover the shortcomings we all have, allowing us to have experiences, learn from them, and grow because of them but not live our entire life condemned that we made a mistake.

Love does not seek out or find fault. Love will overlook imperfection. Love is patient as we live one day to the next trying to navigate not only ourselves but our surroundings that are often bombarded with sin and strife. Love does not afford conflict, worry, or contentions.

Give thanks to the Lord, for He is good; His love endures forever.

—Psalm 106:1

God's love is not with us for a season. God's love is not with us for a day or two. God's love surrounds us all the days of our life. God's love is not conditional. God's love is forever, in good and in bad, all we must do is believe and receive the love of the Lord.

He will not abandon us when we stray from His will. He will not refuse us the pleasure of His Love in any circumstance. There is nothing you can do to make God abandon you; you may walk away from God, but His love for you will remain unchanged all the days of your life.

Love for the Lord is a source of strength and comfort. Your life with the Lord is not necessarily the same as your neighbor's life with the Lord. Each of us grow and mature in Christ throughout our entire lifetime. Don't compare yourself to anyone, don't mimic the actions of others, don't condemn the actions of others. Love others as the Lord loves you.

Above all else love each other deeply.

—1 Peter 4:8

My prayer for you:
Heavenly Father, thank you for the love you allow us to experience. Lord, thank you for the assurance and comfort afforded by Your love. Heavenly Father, thank you for the kindness that comes with the Love of God, the patience that comes with the Love of God, and the peace that comes with the Love of God. Lord Jesus, thank you for remaining ever vigilant by our side, in our hearts, and in our minds. Lord, thank you for the sacrifice of Your Son that we may enjoy the Love of God. Lord, thank you that your Love allows us to remain in your presence day and night, feel the strength and comfort of you, oh Lord, and remain calm amid upheaval. Lord, continue to guide us with your love, forgive us of our sins both knowing and unknowing, and grow us in Love. Amen

CHAPTER 7

Kindness

There is no gesture that is simpler and makes such a lasting impact as that of kindness. Kindness can turn the worst day into the best day, change your mood instantly, and offer hope when you see none. Kindness is both cheap and priceless at the same time! Kindness gives birth to kindness. I have a saying in my writing nook/kitchen table, kindness is never wasted, and it isn't; if it doesn't help the person it was directed toward, it helps the person offering the kindness.

I have a saying posted in my office at my day job: Kindness is common worldwide; I take this to mean kindness is responded to by every individual on the planet in a positive way. It doesn't necessarily mean the other person will respond in kind and certainly doesn't void kindness mistaken for weakness and therefore manipulated and exploited. Kindness can evoke any culture, religion, and race and lead to positive changes and certainly positive outcomes.

At one point, the password on my computer was kindness in abundance; with the remember question as what everyone wants. It takes so little time to smile or to say you look nice, have a great day, or I'm proud of you. The positivity that is spurred from kindness can change the tone of the day, the conversation, or the life of not only children but that of adults as well.

Imagine what the world would be like if every day was World Kindness Day. If you didn't already know as I did not, November 13 is designated World Kindness Day, one of the renowned noted awareness days. The goal of World Kindness Day is to make the world a better place. If we each practice kindness daily, the outcome would be tremendous for both humanity and the environment alike.

Holistic kindness would serve to promote humanity, the environment, and the future for every living thing. So why reserve or limit kindness to once a year. Making kindness a habit would promote oneself daily and consistently and serve as a catalyst to improve the world around us. Simple kindnesses to promote self, other people, and our relationships offers strength and calm, improves mood, and decreases stress. The karma of kindness could soon overtake us if we make the choice to be kind on a regular basis. Give kindness and get kindness in return. Isaiah 55:11 discusses karma of one's actions. What we speak will return to us in kind. Speak kindness, generosity, and mercy get kindness, generosity, and mercy; speak defeat and lack get defeat and lack. Such a small thing to do for self-preservation and such an overlooked attribute of society.

Cultivation of kindness in our daily life will allow us to reap that same kindness we sow as seeds for the future. Ephesians 4:32 explains how God's kindness has forgiven you for all your many transgressions and that we should show kindness toward one another with demonstration of tenderness of heart and forgiveness.

Kindness is an opportunity to change. Change one's self, change another's outlook, change one's faith in mankind, and change the world around us. Kindness given allows kindness to return to us. Kindness changes everything as we know it, a frown to a smile, a defeated mentality to a hopeful future, and a loss to a spark of love and resilience.

Kindness costs nothing and means everything. Kindness exposes your character and is a blessing to both give and receive. The kindness we offer can save a life while offering everlasting importance and promotes self-worth in others. Kindness is strength to both you who is offering the kindness and your brother or sister who is on the receiving end of kindness.

Kindness is wisdom in action and a reflection of your heart. To show kindness, you are showing thoughtfulness, thankfulness, and a genuine sense of caring.

The Bible says kindness is the fruit of the spirit and that kind words are like honey sweet to the soul. Kindness is a choice; kindness counts and is never wasted. Beyond everything else, it is certainly cool to be kind. Practice random acts of kindness and reap the rewards. And don't forget to be kind to yourself.

> A smile or a kind word has more divinity than volumes of religious scripture only read but never lived.
>
> —Luzbek N. Bharucka

God cares for people through people. Actions really do speak louder than words.

My prayer for you:

Heavenly Father, thank you for all that you do and all the kindness offered to us by you. Heavenly Father, thank you for the kindness we project and the lives we improve and touch with kindness. Father, continue to allow us the privilege of strength, growth, and faith in your kindness. Heavenly Father, continue to strengthen us from within and allow us to be graceful when graceful things are not happening to us. Father, thank you that we can remain consistent with our thoughts and actions and not lower ourselves to others poor conceptions of kindness. Father, thank you that we can smile in the presence of ignorance, lack of kindness, and deception. Father, continue to use us to promote kindness in the world and preserve a sense of genuine caring. Amen.

CHAPTER 8

Salvation

Saved by the grace of God! An expression often used by those who believe in Christ or pronounce themselves Christian. Acts 4:12 of the King James Version of the Bible says mankind can be saved by God alone. Salvation is defined as a deliverance from sin or redemption as well as preservation or deliverance from evil or difficulty. Salvation provided by God the Father is all-encompassing deliverance or to be set free or produce the expected and make good. A life lived with the promise of things to come, hope for the future, life after death, and the feeling of living life without fear is salvation and deliverance from the Heavenly Father.

We are saved and offered salvation by God alone; salvation is not attainable without the belief in the Heavenly Father. Christ suffered for us, affording us salvation and provision of peace, life after death, and promises of heaven as discussed in 2 Peter 3:15.

This is salvation that cannot be corrupted, defiled, or withheld due to the ways of the world. Salvation that is everlasting and available with faith. Faith in Jesus Christ/God the Father. Salvation that can never be taken, repealed, or will never be rejected. 1 Peter 1:5 offers the promise of an everlasting never-failing peace with salvation provided by Christ the Lord, King of kings, and Savior of man.

Salvation is as simple as asking God into your life, asking Him to dwell in your heart. It is as simple as believing from that moment on He did come into your heart, save your soul, and started a new budding relationship with Himself Christ the savior. You now have someone 24/7 to talk to, lean on, question, and gain never-ending support from. At the very moment, Christ enters your heart and becomes part of your life you have a promise of life after death, a Heavenly Father, and a relentless friend, amen.

Salvation offers the promise of protection from fear of death (Acts 13:26); fear of the unknown that happens with death. Salvation replaces that fear with life in heaven, life after death, life rejoicing once again with loved ones who have died but were Christ centered and saved by the grace of God now living joyously forevermore in heaven. Salvation is peace in life on earth. Peace that cannot be taken away, revoked, or corrupted by the ways of the world as your salvation from God is not of the world but beyond the world as we know it. This salvation and promise of life after death is waiting for you regardless of the ways of the world, if you chose to believe (Peter 1:5).

Avoid the negativity of nonbelievers as they will try to steal your joy with talk of fairytales, delusions, hallucinations, and fear mongering as they themselves fear and are ignorant of the ways of the Lord. Allow your faith to guide your steps. Be polite and respectful but also be strong and wise as you make your way in a world that is full of multiple religions, gods, and thoughts on humanity.

Remember the history you see and hear is someone else's experience. Seek out your own information so you are not led astray, as sheep being led to slaughter. You should understand you are your own best defense, your one true love. You love and know yourself better and more than anyone ever has. The simple truth is that you must protect your mind, your thoughts, and your personal beliefs. As soon as you are back in the world, the world is done with you; worldly people will ruin your faith, steal your happiness, and walk away unscathed. Ill or no regard for God often leads to jealousy and self-ruin as discussed in Deuteronomy 32:15.

The Redemption offered by God the Father offers a life that is free from further suffering that we may have known on earth. Freedom from worldly heartaches, starvation, devastation, and harm. Revelation 7:10 teaches us that salvation from our Heavenly Father provides us with blessing, thanksgiving, glory, honor, and wisdom beyond our years and that with each of these we can live a life full of dreams, adventure, promise, love, and kindness that nonbelievers do not have.

Salvation from the Lord our God offers us comfort during trying times on earth and peace while we face adversity. It is pleasurable for our Heavenly Father to offer us protection, salvation, promise, and hope. These are attributes of any loving father to his children, fathers and children of every race, religion, creed, nationality, and ethnicity. God the Father provides love and provision to every living thing. It pleases God to provide salvation to His believers that make up the body of Christ: the meek, kind, and faithful.

Once your heart chooses to believe in God as your savior you speak of promises of things to come, life after death, a heavenly reunion with loved ones gone before as you now have hope, hope afforded by the love of God for His children. The Holy Spirit dwells within us, provides constant support, love, and strength as we make our way through life on earth.

It is your trust and belief in God that offers your promise of hope. Life without hope is death, lack, suffering, loneliness, fear, and void of thoughts of a better life or future.

Salvation is the greatest blessing offered by God the Father. Life after death is the salvation of Christ. Salvation provides us with strength from the Lord in troubled times and times of mayhem; instead of chaos and fear, we have peace and hope. Your belief in God the Father and His salvation offers freedom from fear of harm and death.

A happier, more joyous way to live is the promise of God. Happier equals healthier. Healthier equals the possibility of longer and more abundant productive lives.

Salvation offers calm and comfort to our children and any loving father or mother for that matter wants just that for his/her child. Our children need to learn about God the foundation of the world and decide for themselves; salvation must come from within.

> For the Lord and His love endures forever, His faithfulness continues through all generations.
> — Psalm 100:5

My prayer for you:

Heavenly Father, as I am writing to teach and enlighten regarding salvation afforded to each person reading, I pray that every living thing gets the opportunity to enjoy the pleasure that comes with a heart that knows Christ. Lord, please use me, this book, and every other believer to show the simplicity of asking You into one's life. Amen.

If you don't know Jesus Christ as your personal savior, it's as simple as asking Him into your heart and life. There is no right or wrong way, no right or wrong words. Speak out loud, speak in your heart and mind, speak under your breath. Just speak to God, He is Listening, He is waiting. His unconditional love and strength for a joyous happy life, free from fear of death is one word away. Speak to God our Heavenly Father.

CHAPTER 9

Wisdom

I love the term "wisdom of the ages," as I believe it's true. We all grow wiser as we grow older; our experiences, situations, surroundings, environment, and social interactions promote this wisdom. We make decisions later in life that seem smarter and wiser than we did as a child or young adult based on our experiences and knowledge that continuously grows and evolves throughout our lifespan.

Albeit, I have, as I am sure you have, heard the expression some people never learn, well they don't, they continuously make poor choices throughout their entire life that may result in imprisonment, impoverished lifestyle, and abuse or disruptive situations that never seem to resolve. It's possible these people have no positive influence in their lives; this is what they have seen, endured, or what has been modeled to them, so they act as others in their life have acted. Rest assured more than not they are not followers of Christ and have had very little influence from those who love the Lord our God.

Research proves that those with more motherly attention and love for the first six weeks of life endure less anxiety, stress, and experience better health and wellness later in life. This means the way you were treated the first six weeks of your life dominates your mentality until you are aged and reach the end of your life.

This is the same for Christ our Lord, when He is presented to us as children, we lose the fear of death, we understand we are always loved, friended, supported, and strengthened. We can reach out to Christ at any time and He is always there ready to lend an ear, helping hand, or shoulder to cry on. Those with the Heavenly Father's influence understand that they can seek His wisdom for decision making, trust His timing, and enjoy His support in undesirable situations; ultimately promoting happiness, wellness, and life.

Believe it or not, I got a daily devotional from Joel Osteen today and I will paraphrase: wise people follow the wise if you hang around fools to long you become foolish yourself. I get these devotionals daily and I am sure he did not know my current chapter as I have not told anyone I am writing, and this is the subject for today. Furthermore, I live in Indiana, not Texas, but the Lord knows I attend via television, radio, and other social media. It's the hand of the Lord I am sure of it telling me to continue. Telling me I am supported, heard, understood, and will help someone come to know Him as I do. This was my word from God strengthening my own decision making and showing me wisdom in my own personal choices and the things and people I chose to have in my life. I get a daily devotional from Osteen ministries and have for years; this was not coincidence. This was God the Heavenly Father supporting me as my endeavor of writing this book is only half realized at this moment.

Proverbs 3:13 teaches us happiness with the wisdom and understanding of God as we are no longer searching or feeling the emptiness and lack of hope that is in a life without our Heavenly Father. Truth through wisdom allows us to search for meaning to what we do and seek beyond the surface or a superficial trait.

A wise individual will seek counsel in decision making using the experience of another to help guide and support decision making Daniel 5:11. Searching meaning, truth, and guidance will help us to avoid mistakes, poor choices, and falsities that surround us every day as we make our way through the world. Happiness is what we all seek to find, and happiness can simply be found daily in our walk with God.

With wisdom is discretion and smart decision making that leads us on a productive path and allows us to enjoy a well spent life with a promise and hope of life after death. We walk in light and happiness instead of darkness and fear with the wisdom of our Heavenly Father.

Advancements in the home, finances, family, and self are supported by wisdom (Matthew 12:42).

The wisdom of the Lord teaches us, prospers us, and allows us to grow. Do not be deceived as you search for goodness and wisdom, learn to recognize and trust your instincts and gut feelings if something just does not feel right. As you reflect on situations, talk to God, ask him to reveal the truth, as to what was wrong and caused your unrest.

Do not be hasty in decision making, contemplate, and remember snakes and misguidance are everywhere and disguise themselves to appear appealing all the while trying to corrupt and cause harm. Heathens are without wisdom and the word of God and seek to destroy and cause havoc with disregard for the Holy Spirit.

Wisdom and knowledge allow for change within our heart, mind, and spirit, and as it is taking place, you sense it with increased understanding, willingness to be open-minded, forgiving, loving, and kind. These changes are apparent both inward and outward for the world to see and take notice. Christ seekers often demonstrate wisdom in truth and are guided by conscience. A conscience that promotes truth, patience, sincerity, and love in abundance. Wisdom equals goodness as discussed in James 3:15.

> She opens her mouth in wisdom and the teachings of kindness is upon her tongue.
> —Proverbs 31:26

A wise person will seek knowledge and learning to increase himself and his own knowledge and understanding and will listen intently, abundantly, and with interest. When we seek wisdom from the Lord our Heavenly Father, we are not limiting ourselves to our own understanding and learning we are expanding our minds, hearts, and level of understanding. It has been said everyone can teach us something and the Lord our Heavenly Father supports this with a discussion of conceited thinking and feeling as if we know it all and have nothing left to learn (Proverbs 1:15, 3:7).

As our earthly father teaches us, our Heavenly Father wants us to learn and teach our children demonstrating His wisdom to our young. Teaching our children will place them on a path to correctness leading to productivity, encouraging faith in God and decreasing strife and fear from death with words of heaven and life after death (Luke 1:17).

By teaching our children and seeking knowledge ourselves, we are practicing wisdom with faith in God. Wisdom that allows us to increase our knowledge of the Lord, the world, and walk a more abundant path throughout our lifespan. A life free from the burden of poor choices, bad decision making, and mistakes that haunt and remind us daily of our imperfections. Seeking the Heavenly Father and his wisdom is a choice and a chance to wash away the old and start a new, fresh, and happy life. Trusting in the wisdom of the Lord who created the heavens and the earth will allow you to live free from the past (Proverbs 3:19; Ephesians 1:8).

With continued seeking of Christ our Heavenly Father, we will increase our understanding of language, actions, and needs; we will be afforded wisdom in knowledge and discretion in our own actions. Wisdom from God allows us to listen and learn, speak wisdom and truths in the natural as they are provided to us by the heart of our Heavenly Father. Fools lack wisdom and despise the wise who offer instruction.

> For the Lord gives wisdom and from His mouth
> comes knowledge and understanding.
> —Proverbs 2:6

Seek God and bring Him into your life. Ask God for wisdom and guidance. God will never refuse to help you; God the Heavenly Father is help for those who help themselves as discussed in James 1:5.

The mighty wisdom of God is ready to be shared, all we need to do is reach out, search for our Heavenly Father, invite Him into our heart as He loves us all the same. No one carries more favor with

God than you do. All you must do is seek Him. Wisdom is strength, honor, glory, and blessing provided by our Heavenly Father.

My prayer for you:

Heavenly Father, as we come to You once more, let us thank You for the wisdom You bestow upon us every day. Heavenly Father, thank You for always being available when we seek counsel, never refusing us Your presence. Lord, thank you for the abundance of knowledge and wisdom you show the world daily to allow your creations to evolve and thrive in an ever-changing environment of hosts, ideas, thoughts, and creative actions. Lord, continue to promote Yourself in us by improving our wisdom and showing Yourself in our decision making, actions, and thoughts. Heavenly Father, thank You for providing each of us with an inward compass that we call a conscience to guide us along our daily paths and prosper and promote us in love, understanding, kindness, and wisdom. Amen.

CHAPTER 10

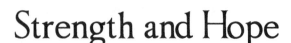

Strength and Hope

I don't know how often I say the words, "Lord, give me strength." Strength for whatever is going on in my life. Strength and heavenly guidance, support, and hope to endure and attend to life's daily and never-ending problems. The Lord did not promise a life without problems and trials, but He did promise a life with endless support and strength from Himself if we just ask.

Ask God for the strength to endure, carry on, and make the right decisions regardless how large or small the problem or trial may seem. The Heavenly Father is there for you and for me alike because we believe. We need not make a scene asking for help, we can quietly whisper in our heart, souls, and minds to God and seek His strength in times of trouble.

When we have exhausted our strength, God offers hope (Romans 5:6). Hope provides a chance at something better, something to cling to when we feel helpless, and something to dream about when our situation is dire and dark. Hope is the light at the end of the tunnel, the clear-headed thoughts after months of muddling through to make sense, and hope is the way forward into the future you desire.

There is a sense of security that hope offers, a place to rest knowing there are possibilities for something better to come and is certainly possible if we believe. Hope offered by the Heavenly Father is happiness and help for all those who choose to believe in the Holy Spirit.

We can find the hope offered by Christ in the word of God, prayers, and scriptures. We can find hope in patience with others and ourselves when we are undergoing an evolutionary period in our lives. Hope allows for forward thinking and the opportunity to learn from the past knowing there is a future that has the potential to be brighter and outshine anything in our past if we believe, strive, and do not give up or become defeated as we seek out the desires of our heart.

> Faith, Hope, and Love. But the greatest is love.
> —1 Corinthians 13:13

With the Lord, we enjoy faith for what we cannot see, hope to believe for better, charity and kindness to love and support one another throughout life. Hope provides for mindfulness of things to come. Hope offers the thoughts of reaping what you sow; invest in yourself with hope for a future that would not be possible without the love and will of God.

Hope is a blessing to live justly knowing the Heavenly Father is there to strengthen and help when He is called upon and He is always willing to listen. Hope is demonstrated in the lives of our ancestors who came before and experienced God's mercy in healing, struggles, and human advancement as we know it. The founding fathers of the United States were so profound in their beliefs of Christ they printed every paper currency to state "In God We Trust," they were given the promise land they had hoped for. Their dreams and desires were given to them because they acted. The ability to worship Christ as they felt compelled was the driving force behind America as we know it. The moment they believed in the Heavenly Father they had hope for a better life, a better situation, and faith strong enough to seek their desired future.

Hope belongs to those who know Christ the moment they come to know Him and His never-ending love. The Lord is hope, and without God, there is no hope, no hope for a better future, no hope for life after death, and no hope for better days. Life without hope is dismay and destruction. Hope is for the living only; once we are dead, it is too late. The resurrection of Christ demonstrated hope of life after death and better things to come without fear and misery of the unknown of death.

We can see God in ourselves as we express hope of better things to come. Patience and experience equal hope; there is no shame in hope as we need to have experience to grow and evolve as humans and as believers (Romans 5:4).

The hope of Christ is the glory of heaven as promised.

> Be strong and take heart, all you who hope in
> the Lord.
> — Psalm 31:24

My prayer for you:

Heavenly Father, thank you for not only the glimmer of hope you afford humanity but the shining light and comfort you bring to those of us who choose to believe in the possibility of a life after death. A heaven, a reunion with those gone on before, and a life free from suffering and death. Thank you, Heavenly Father, for the comfort that comes with hope and the joy of a hopeful tomorrow. Christ Jesus, continue to provide comfort and strength through hope as we make our way through this life on earth. Lord Jesus, teach, lead, and guide us that we may offer hope to the lost and lonely who are suffering and to those without a personal relationship with you.

Amen.

CHAPTER 11

Prayer

Prayer is not just words spoken but is the communication we share with our Heavenly Father. I speak to God as if He is right there beside me all the time. When we pray to God, we don't have to make a scene and pray so others can hear, we must simply and mindfully address our wants, concerns, needs, and desires to the Lord in thought. Second Samuel 7:27 suggests we pray and ask God for what we want, the desires of our heart that we do not readily share with others.

The Heavenly Father sees our heart and knows our mind. He is waiting for us to ask for that house, car, loved one to heal or recover, and He will respond in kind. Nothing is too large or too small for our Heavenly Father. Do not minimize your dreams and desires; that is why they are your dreams and desires. The Lord has placed them in your heart or mine not to be determined by those around us who may think we are crazy or delusional, but for us to dream as big as we like. Act on your dreams and make them a reality with effort, trial and failure, and never giving up but leaning on our Heavenly Father when the world around us is thinking small.

Do not allow another individual who may have a negative mindset, lack of experience, and limited personal beliefs drive your life. It is your life to live and your dreams to dream so pray for what you want, what you desire most, and then work toward it. The Lord helps those who help themselves; your own personal efforts will make all the difference in your success.

Mark 11:24 tells us we should believe that our prayers will be answered, and we will receive the things we requested from our Heavenly Father. We must put actions to words and work toward our prayers. Trust in the Lord, your Heavenly Father, to provide the desires of your heart once you ask for them. It may not be on your timetable, your exact expectation, and your way but pray to God to help you make your dreams reality.

Pray for patience to see your dreams through, regardless of the trials and failures, the naysayers, and the often-resentful people in your life who manifest as family and friends. It is not uncommon for those closest to you to not want you to succeed and become more than they are themselves, as this takes away from their self-importance. Matthew 5:44 suggests you pray for these deceitful individuals who do not know how to pray for themselves.

Everyone will not be for you, but you can pray for them to someday come to know God and find resolution for themselves so they can celebrate and promote others. You cannot pray and gain salvation for another, you can only show them the way to a relationship with our Heavenly Father. A relationship that would allow them to pray their own bold prayers and open their mind to the true desires of their heart.

We are none perfect and our Heavenly Father will not deny your prayers for forgiveness; ask for forgiveness of sin and move on, do not dwell on the past it is only a stop toward your future. Pray anytime day or night, in bed, in your car, in your shower, while working, doing dishes, shoveling dirt—just pray there is nothing so great our Heavenly Father will not help with.

The Holy Spirit will lead your path if you simply reach out in prayer. Romans 8:2 teaches us that the Spirit of God will help with prayer and praise. Cry out to God in prayer that He may hear your voice and your praises alike. Pray for afflictions and praise justice, kindness, love, charity, mercy, merriment, safety, and contentment as discussed in James 5:13.

For with God nothing shall be impossible.
—Luke 1:37

Pray that others may come to know your Heavenly Father and prosper. Pray for peace for nations and people alike. Pray knowing the Lord hears you because you believe. Show you believe by putting actions to your prayers. Furthermore, if the Lord puts it in your heart act on it. Don't boast as to make another jealous or promote envious behavior but do make others aware of your already answered prayers. Share your thoughts and prayers with others as this may be the path that leads them to Christ our Heavenly Father.

Luke 16:27 tells us to pray for the needs of others. Your love of the Lord should be visible to anyone you encounter, no need to state it demonstrate it. I have a small sign in my dining room that reads "A good example is the best sermon"; this is not only true for a pastor or sermon this is true for all of us. You never really know who is watching taking their cue about God and faith from you and your actions. Pray for others to have strength and comfort regardless of the situation. Teach others to pray as a source of comfort and strength as you journey through this life on earth.

Pray for spiritual gifts that will help you lead others to Christ and demonstrate His will and grow you in Christ. Use your prayer life as an example of your commitment to our Heavenly Father. Use prayer to promote others, soothe the savage, calm the anxious, and heal the wounded.

Pray every day. Prayer is not work it is counsel with our Heavenly Father. Never stop praying, if you miss a day, a week, or a month as you make your way through life there is no rule that you cannot go back and rekindle God's spirit in you; He is waiting to answer your prayers and be part of your life.

My prayer for you:

Heavenly Father, please allow me to pray today so that others may come to know You, feel Your presence in their lives, and find grace and comfort in Your words. Heavenly Father, thank you for being forever present in my heart. Heavenly Father, thank you that with simple prayer I am fortunate enough to enjoy your blessings, your promises of things to come, your strength, and hedge of protection in my life.

Heavenly Father, continue to allow me to promote Your goodness in prayer. Heavenly Father, allow my actions and my words to touch those around me who do and do not believe in the power of prayer that they may see your goodness daily.

Amen.

CHAPTER 12

Church

Church doesn't have to be a million-dollar sanctuary; church can be your current space in a crowded elevator. Anyplace you choose to praise the Lord, your Heavenly Father, is church. Church is a place set aside to worship; churchgoers are worshipers who share similar beliefs and attend the same church.

Church congregations are just that, groups of people with the same or similar beliefs who come together to worship in their fashion with their set of ideas. The church or congregation is also considered the body of Christ. For Christians, the Heavenly Father is the head and the church and congregation therefore are the body of Christ.

The Bible doesn't say church has to be directed by any one individual, it does however speak of the preacher offering a sermon and seeking wisdom from the elders. Therefore, you could have your own church as it fits your certain needs if you are congregated or alone praising in the name of Christ, it is church. Don't be misled by the unjust, self-satisfying among you whom try to lead you astray. Always trust yourself and your relationship with God when it comes to worship. There is no one person closer to God than yourself.

Your chosen church should be built on a solid foundation with the Heavenly Father at the center of everything offering solid beliefs and never wavering trust. This doesn't have to be surrounded by any certain type of dwelling this has to come from within as discussed in Matthew 16:18.

Your chosen church and congregation should be open and welcoming, forgiving, offer support and guidance grounded in unconditional love as the love of the Heavenly Father is also unconditional.

Don't allow another's beliefs and disgraces or actions to keep you from praising God the Heavenly Father for if you do the only one who will suffer is you. You will lose precious time with your Heavenly Father, lose His support and unconditional love in your life, lose His strength and His joy while the doubter goes about unaffected.

It is perfectly normal to want to seek out and find a place to feel as if you fit in and have the same ideas and beliefs as the rest of the worshiping congregation. Your parents' church or your grandparents' church may not be the best place for you and that is okay—find your own place of worship where God the Heavenly Father is the center of everything.

A church, if you will, is your chosen destination to praise and worship your heavenly father as He intended His children do when they attend and congregate in His name. And never forget the Lord says He is there where one or two congregate. He doesn't say unless you have a thousand people in a building that costs millions, I'm not coming! He is with you always just seek Him and do not be dismayed by numbers and thoughts of others.

We should be trying to add to the body/church of Christ every day by our actions our discussion and our own praises. We should be willing to accept others into the church, teaching them of our Heavenly Father and seeking His favor in doing so as stated in Acts 2:47. The church is a place to praise God and we should be leading people to praise God with a relationship with the Heavenly Father. A relationship that is either personal and private or public and open it makes no difference, but actions should match the words coming from your tongue.

This doesn't mean we will never have a bad day; this means we do the best we can to our understanding and realize each person has a different understanding of Christ the Heavenly Father and a different relationship with Him. We may lose our temper, we may say something we know we should not, we may act as many of His human disciples did because we are just that, human!

Be quick to forgive yourself as the Lord is quick to forgive. Gain wisdom from mistakes and move forward in Christ as He wants you to grow as we watch our earthly children grow. Perfection is not an aspiration of our Heavenly Father, a relationship of love and trust, faith and belief are what He is seeking in His children.

The place you choose to call your church and to worship the Lord our Heavenly Father should be a place of love, comfort, and knowledge (1 Corinthians 4:17); if you do not have these at your church, search another until you are among your Heavenly Father's children. Never discount your gut so to speak as this is your conscience telling you something is not right and remember the Lord speaks to us through our conscience. Each of us is born with an essence of right and wrong that comes from our Heavenly Father. What is right for you may not be right for another; don't judge, just don't participate.

Church should offer you wisdom of your Heavenly Father as discussed in Ephesians 3:10. Seek your Heavenly Father in church, seek answers to your questions, seek a closer relationship with your Heavenly Father, and seek love and joy offered by your Heavenly Father in church. Praise and uplift the name of the Heavenly Father in church. The church is a place to teach the word of God and to Love the Lord.

You should also expect persecution for your beliefs in Christ our Heavenly Father. Persecution for your love of God. And furthermore persecution of the church which is the body of Christ. Not everyone is evolved enough to accept the differences we all share and will potentially lash out at what they don't understand, what they desire, and what they cannot control.

A little history, did you know that the term church was formulated after the followers of Christ had assembled themselves for a year or more to worship and praise God. An assembly of praises was the first church. It was not a large building, a day to dress in your best, or a formal celebration.

Oftentimes, throughout the Bible, the assembly of the Heavenly Father's followers were disruptive, they expressed doubts, and they acted out in their fear and frustration, but they were quickly forgiven, set forth on the right path, and remained in the congregation to form the body of Christ. None were perfect, they were believers in the Heavenly Father and His promises.

My prayer for you:

Heavenly Father, as we come before you once again, please hear our prayer today; it is a prayer of understanding and wisdom. Heavenly Father, do not allow Your children to be led astray, persecuted, and forgotten because they feel they are not part of a formal societal brand of church. Heavenly Father, allow your children the wisdom to know they can reach out to you and assemble among themselves, assemble alone in prayer, and worship when and where it is needed. Heavenly Father, we pray today for love and joy that is offered by You and Your presence in Church. Heavenly Father, be with each believer as they work daily to grow Your church.

Amen.

CHAPTER 13

Grace

"By the grace of God," we have all heard it, we may have said it, but do you really understand it? Grace from your Heavenly Father is a quality of good character, pleasing and kind, good will, and mercy toward others. Mercy that forgives previous actions and allows another to move forward in life without having to relive the past and past mistakes over and over because of someone else's ignorance and lack of grace and forgiveness.

The grace we enjoy from our Heavenly Father is a divine grace full of love and protection that is given freely by God the Father. Grace is dignified behavior, behavior that is of good quality, loving, and kind. Grace is humble and loving toward another and kind with another's heart, demonstrated by wholesome, loving, and understanding words and actions.

Grace provided by our Heavenly Father fills us with wisdom and love toward one another. Grace is a gift from God. Grace is truth. Grace is given and grace is received in kind (karma of grace if you will). Grace promotes goodness as discussed in Colossians 1:6.

God was so graceful toward His followers and believers that He allowed by mercy His son to be crucified and made to experience death so that we as followers of Christ may live and experience life after death and heaven. Hebrews 2:9 discusses how our Heavenly Father, by grace, allowed us to live and have the hope of life after death.

With the belief of God and by His grace, we are saved. Grace allows us to enjoy hope of a life after death in which we will rejoice in heaven with God the Heavenly Father and our loved ones who believed, were faith filled, and have died and gone on to be with the Lord our God in heaven.

With grace from the Lord, we are protected in Christ and have Satan/the devil under our feet not about us stirring up trouble and strife. With grace, strength, and protection from Christ we can say to Satan depart from me, devil get behind me, or in Jesus's name devil stop and it has to be as a promise from our Heavenly Father; just say it, believe it, and it will be (Romans 16:20).

From the moment you accept our Heavenly Father into your life, you are surrounded by His protection and engulfed in His mighty grace and wisdom. The grace of God is with you in every situation from that moment when you accept Him as your Lord and Savior and invite Him into your heart and mind. The grace of God is simple and pure as discussed in Philippians 4:23. Our Heavenly Father's grace is more than enough for every individual in every situation; we are all His beings, His children, and His desire is to be good to us.

Seek the Heavenly Father to provide you with calm in chaos. Seek the Heavenly Father to offer hope for future offenses we are all going to commit. Seek the Heavenly Father to allow you to witness the grace of God in those around you. Ask the Heavenly Father to fill you with His spirit of grace, to bring you happiness in tears, peace in trials, comfort, strength, support, and stability all the days of your life (Acts 11:23).

Seek God's grace to provide you with peaceful solutions in times of great conflict. Seek God's grace to not harbor hate and vengeance but love and kindness in all situations. However hard that may be, you need to do it for your own emotional health because the person causing the hate and bitterness will only be promoted and enjoy triumph at your expense as long as you allow them in your life and to manipulate your emotions and feelings.

I am learning a lesson in God's grace as I am writing this and seeking calm, grace, and quietness when my internet service is blocked, manipulated, and disrupted, causing me to have delays, get unwanted content, and not get expected content. I have been a child of God from a very tender age and continue to struggle with temperament and trying to rationalize someone else's poor decisions, ignorance, and lack of scruples daily. So do not fault yourself if you struggle and stumble in some area of your walk with your Heavenly Father, He already knows you are not perfect, but He also knows of your love for Him and that you are trying.

Thank and praise your Heavenly Father daily, thank Him for His never-ending support and love. Thank Him for His wisdom and calm in times of devastation and chaos. Ask Him to help you become more accepting of others. Seek the wisdom and grace of the Heavenly Father to be comforted in times of sorrow.

Seek the grace of the Heavenly Father to always forgive and help us deal with our anger that we may exhibit, experience, and bestow on others. Just ask Him to forgive you in times of these less graceful actions and believe He did and move on. It matters not how many people remember and try to bring it to you as ammunition to hold you back or keep you down; what matters is God the Father put it behind you and His opinion is the only opinion you should be worried about when it comes to your salvation.

With grace from your Heavenly Father, you also find understanding in His word and His desires to promote and protect you. God the Heavenly Father remains in your conscience steering your steps; He Himself is always with you and His grace abides in you as well. There are multiple chapters of the Bible that simply state grace with you always in every situation: awake, sleeping, ill, well, troubled, happy, content, tested, fear, and joy. Simply grace is with you. Own your Heavenly Father's grace and practice it daily as it makes Him proud to promote and prosper His children.

The spirit of our Heavenly Father lives within us despite death. We as believers in Christ our Heavenly Father project the grace of God into the world around us, abundantly filling those around us with love, kindness, the word of the Lord, and demonstrating patience, hope, understanding, and eternal grace.

Clothe yourselves with compassion, kindness, humility, gentleness and patience.
— Colossians 3:12

Compassion, kindness, humility, gentleness, and patience are all attributes of grace and the Heavenly Father; demonstrations of His love and grace abound when we practice these.

My prayer for you:

Heavenly Father, forgive us our transgressions; our less graceful moments that cause you shame and us emotional upheaval that is not necessary and not what You desire for your children to experience. Heavenly Father, thank you for never leaving nor forsaking us and providing us with your endless grace, compassion, comfort, and indwelling spirit to guide and direct our paths. Heavenly Father, help each of us to be more like You and demonstrate your grace toward others on a regular basis in every given situation, whether right or wrong, happy or sad, troubled or content allow us to remain steadfast in your grace, oh Heavenly Father, I pray.

Amen.

CHAPTER 14

Trust and Belief

Trust in the Lord our Heavenly Father with all your heart as He hears your cry and wants to be in your life. Free will allows you to decide if you want Him there, want His guidance and His comfort. Free will created by the Heavenly Father is a testimony to His trust in us that He will be there. He will provide as promised and protect us if we believe and seek Him in our daily lives.

There is no difference in believing and having faith Romans 3:22 of the original King James Version of the Bible. Our faith is projected when we believe. We believe in the Heavenly Father and our actions support this belief with kindness, love, forgiveness, and charity that we bestow on others around us daily. We may not always realize what we are doing, we often act out of need, but when we act on something, it is of a promising and promotional uplifting nature that is supported by our Heavenly Father.

There is no certain word to ask God to come into your heart. Your belief in God saves you without words. If you are called to act on and support your faith with more than words, your actions of belief will save you, allowing your soul a life after death with the Heavenly Father as discussed in Romans 10:9. Believe Christ was raised from the dead to go beyond the clouds to a heavenly home to live with God the Father.

Evil believes and fears your Heavenly Father. Allow your actions to project outward to the world your faith in our Heavenly Father and don't get discouraged with setbacks as we all are human and react as humans; control of emotion, thoughts, and reactions take time. Mature in Christ, don't doubt or give up, grow in Christ's everlasting love for His children. He doesn't seek perfection He seeks believers to join Him in a life after death.

Do not succumb to a life of foolishness, testing God's love for you. Seeking signs, doubting, and demanding behaviors will not allow your soul to rest and reside with the Heavenly Father. To the contrary, it will cause you strife as you struggle within yourself to find inner peace, tranquility, and the awesome unrelenting love of the Heavenly Father. Believe in the saving of the soul. Belief equals faith, faith equals salvation.

2 Corinthians 4:3 tells us to speak what we believe. If you believe in your Heavenly Father, speak it. Declare your love of God. Be a witness for the Heavenly Father and the goodness He has allowed you to enjoy.

Speak of the peace He has placed in your heart, a heart free of worry and strife, free of fear and death. Speak of the hedge of protection promised by our Heavenly Father if we believe. Speak of your long talks with God. Speak of His goodness and faithfulness, readiness to listen each time you reach out to Him. Speak of the wondrous love your Heavenly Father has surrounded you with. Speak of the hope provided by your belief in the Heavenly Father.

Promote good works for your Heavenly Father, do not seek your validation from others as you will be displeased. Validation from the world is conditional on meeting demands, being of the crowd, fitting in with the group, going along with the wrong thing when you know you should be doing what is right and right with your Heavenly Father. Worldly validation keeps you seeking approval from those around you. Seek approval and validation from your Heavenly Father only, not the world. Be respectful of other opinions but realize you don't have to have them in your life.

Don't allow people to hold you back. Don't allow conversations of people whom you don't know to hold you back. Do not allow others to steal your future. Do not allow the jealousy of another person to hold you back from the wonderful, prosperous, and faith-filled peaceful life your Heavenly Father has for you.

Blessed is the one who trusts in the Lord.
— Jeremiah 17:7

Seek validation from your Heavenly Father only and keep moving forward. The Lord helps those who help themselves. This doesn't mean be reckless and put yourself in harm's way, this means do not fear what comes naturally, protect yourself and your heart from the outside world, and lean on the Heavenly Father for his guidance. As a believer, you have a lifeline to your Heavenly Father use it often as He desires to be good to you, protect you, and validate you. Believe and trust your Heavenly Father in every aspect of your life; nothing is too large or too small for your Heavenly Father.

Heaven is faith's promise to believers; don't give that up with doubts and fears, hold steady to your Heavenly Father. Believe with all your heart that Jesus is the Son of God and was resurrected to live in heaven and provide you a way out of death's darkness to reside in heaven as well. Believers exemplify charity, faith, purity of heart, and peace within the spirit. Show your belief in your faith with your conversations and your discussion of the word of God.

My prayer for you:
Heavenly Father Loving and Kind, Heavenly Father Wise and Divine, thank you for allowing us to come before you another day to praise and worship you in our beliefs. Our beliefs that are a choice we make and not a mandate to action. Lord, thank you for the free will You bestow upon us to make our own decisions, mistakes, and promises. Thank you for the opportunity to believe and seek a place for our soul to reside with You in heaven, once again meeting and enjoying loved ones who also chose to believe. Lord, thank you for the peace, kindness, and love that comes with believing in our Heavenly Father. Lord, thank you for the constant companion we have in You if we only believe.
Amen.

CHAPTER 15

Heaven

Genesis 1:1 tells how our Heavenly Father created the heavens and the earth; the firmament (expanse of heaven-the sky). Our Heavenly Father created the great expanse called the earth and the heavens along with the separation of the dry lands from the sea. If studied, you would be able, as if you were doing a puzzle in your home, to identify where the earth's continents were potentially as one. With time and the natural evolutionary process of changes that occur to adapt to the environment, note where we are today in the world as it relates to geography.

The heavens provide light that designates day and night. Light from the sun that is in the orbit of the earth making every condition known to man be able to survive and thrive; nothing else like it known to man in our solar system.

No sister planet as to compare, no distant neighbor to watch grow and develop, and no accompanying system of agriculture, heat, cold, night, day, perfect gravitational pull, and environment suitable to sustain life as we know it! We have a perfect moon that arises from the heavens at night to note and light the darkness unlike any other planet in our known solar system. With light and dark, seasons of warmth and cold, regeneration in the spring after a cold barren winter in which the environment goes dormant to only come alive again in another season under our heaven; unlike anything we know and unlike anyone else we know experiences.

Our Heavenly Father created a place for us to dwell that would suit our needs and allow us to thrive as a mirror image of Himself and His needs. He supplied everything for life to sustain itself in the image of Him our Heavenly Father.

Evolutionary measures allow for change to occur so we can adapt, maintain, thrive, and survive in our environments as they change. The ape still exists, the fish, the fowl, the tortoise, the whale, the lion and we have extinction as well, but the son of man remains unchanged He has not evolved and has not become extinct. His knowledge grows, but his image remains the same.

It's your decision regarding your belief of heaven and the Heavenly Father; it is a decision of hope, happiness, and good things to come. When making this decision, do not allow anyone to skew your thoughts based on their negative opinions, experiences, and bitterness. Seek and find hope in heaven and in your Heavenly Father.

The heavens are perfect and never ending. There is no dividing line from the north and south hemisphere, no breaks in continuity across the sky, just a perfect circumference surrounding the earth as far as the eye can see and the imagination can fathom. Perfection in the heavens is never ending.

Doubt of heaven is as old as time itself. Great wars in the name of religion as well as death and suffering in the name of religion all litter our history, but the perfection of the heavens remains the same. We see God in the light of day, in the beauty of the stars at night, and in the moon that sheds its light on us to light our darkness.

Perfect sequencing of the rotation of the heavens and the earth. "To everything there is a season, and a time to every purpose under the Heaven" (Ecclesiastes 3:1 KJV).

All under heaven are creatures of the Heavenly Father, His house if you will. Praise and thank Him for His creation. A creation that is so perfect that it allows us as the image of Him to reside, thrive, and enjoy the luxuries He has set forth for us.

Praise your Heavenly Father and do good until the day He chooses for the earth to pass and cease to exist as we know it. Praise and thank Him for the promise of life in the heavens with Him. A life free of pain, sorrow, tears, strife, and death. Heaven is a place to refresh and renew, free of worldly sorrow, shame, fear, doubt, sickness, oppression, and the unknown.

Many of us experience heaven in visions, in our dreams, in our mind, and find the comfort of God our Heavenly Father in these dreams and visions. Cling to them and do not be dismayed by what is going on in the world around you but find peace and joy in God's heaven.

My prayer for you:

Heavenly Father, thank you for the vision of heaven. Thank you for the promise and hope of things to come. Heavenly Father, thank you for the beauty of the heavens in the daylight and in the night. Thank you for the perfection of the sun to warm the days and the soft glow of the moon to light the nights that would otherwise be too cold to endure. Heavenly Father, thank you for the stars in the heaven, the light and beauty they hold. Heavenly Father, thank you that we live on a star that is habitable due to your love and compassion when the rest of what we know is a cosmic void free of life as we know it on earth. Heavenly Father, thank you for the beauty of life.

Amen.

CHAPTER 16

Grief, Strife, Sorrow, and Hate

Our Heavenly Father wants us to walk in love and sees us as His dear children. He does not want us to grieve for Him who died upon the cross but to have hope of life after death. Our Heavenly Father wants us to live in peace, comfort, and feel His protective spirit in our day to day lives.

Our Heavenly Father wants us to live beyond bitterness, anger, hate, and evil as this will only cause us grief and strife; God wants us to recognize these things for what they are but not to dwell upon them and not give them time in our spirit.

Grieve for a season as natural; do not waste your life grieving for something that happened that you had no control over, you could not change, and you were not responsible for. Grief helps no one, grief produces nothing positive, and grief is not good for the soul. Grief comes in many forms; do not grieve for misbehaving children, obtuse employers, or unsatisfying positions in life. Instead, praise God your child is coming toward the right path. Praise God you have a job to pay your bills while searching for the job you truly desire. Furthermore, praise God that He is making a path for you to advance to new heights in life. Praise God that he is providing you with the secret desires of your heart.

Strife, grief, hatred, and envy are not led by the Holy Spirit; recognize this and do not allow it to dwell in your heart and overtake your mind. Disregard those who preach and teach strife from God our Heavenly Father as these are not attributes of the Holy Spirit.

Give credit where credit is due, recognize your fellow man for all his ideas, strengths, comforts, his love for our Heavenly Father, and his actions. I believe the saying that you can get a tremendous amount of good accomplished if you do not care who gets the credit. Some people are motivated only by recognition of others and will only act if they are the driving force and more important than another.

Your idea in someone else's hands may save millions of lives, produce the next generation of faith-filled children, or promote your congregation to a new level. Unselfishness is pure love of your Heavenly Father.

Be aware ignorance is proud of knowing nothing, boasting, doting, and railing from envy promoting strife, but this is not of the Heavenly Father. Love, compassion, patience, support, and comfort are from the Heavenly Father and attributes of faith, not ways to seek glory from man. Strife ends when salvation begins Hebrews 6:16. Envy and strife cause confusion, chaos, and evil.

Sorrow comes with foul deeds and actions, remorse, regret, and punishment.

Sorrow results from not following your Heavenly Father's path for you and results in trembling, fear, and heavy heartedness. Lack of rest, uneasiness with action, and no direction are expressed as sorrow. It is impossible to hide sorrow as it is expressed in your daily conversations, decisions, and overall well-being.

When you have sorrow, your enemy has the power over you but only you can give them this power by allowing strife, envy, chaos, and hate into your life. Declare to your Heavenly Father your sorrow and move on, stop the sorrow by sharing it with your Heavenly Father and seek His forgiveness and guidance and move forward. Mischief leads to sorrow so distance yourself from it, from mischief makers, and mischief supporters. No hope is sorrow.

This must be one of the hardest things I have read and am working on accepting as I am sure it is not easy for anyone to love someone who hates you. The Heavenly Father teaches that it takes more patience, kindness, and character to have compassion and charity for those who do not know Him and who hate you for your relationship with Him. Our Heavenly Father wants us to demonstrate

His love for all His creatures by loving those who hate us for one reason or another. The Heavenly Father wants us to pray for those that harbor hate, that they may come to know Him and experience His all-encompassing love and compassion for His children.

Do not be sorrowful when people hate you, envy you, and lie to and about you, exclude you, and try to discredit you; it reflects them and their character and not you. Rejoice that you have the love of your Heavenly Father and regardless of what someone else thinks, you are free to make your own way, set your own goals, and live life to the fullest knowing you are loved, comforted, protected, and blessed by the Heavenly Father.

Hatred will not endure; it will be exposed by overwhelming emotion and strife. Hate will expose itself for what it is, ungodly and unworthy of any form of your time or attention. The actions of hatred speak louder than the words of a true hater. They may express love on the outward but secretly hate and try to undermine what they envy on the inside; this will reveal itself as they will not be happy harboring such feelings. Hatred has no eternal life, no hope, no promise of heaven, and no comfort from the Heavenly Father.

My prayer for you:

Heavenly Father, continue to be with us, lead, guide, and direct our paths. Heavenly Father, thank you for removing any semblance of hate, sorrow, and strife from our lives. Heavenly Father, thank you for the understanding that grief is not to be lived daily. Grief is to be experienced with our losses but not relived repeatedly. Heavenly Father, thank you for strength and comfort to deal with those who possess hatred, sorrow, grief, and strife. Heavenly Father, continue to shroud us with your hedge of protection that allows us to live life to the fullest unharmed by the hate, strife, sorrow, and grief of others.

Amen.

CHAPTER 17

Patience, Peace, and Resurrection

To be patient is to be tolerant and understanding; patience is remaining calm under trying times and circumstances. A person who practices patience is consistent, persevering in every situation, and one who can calmly await an outcome without hastily reacting. A patient person will calmly collect all the information and endure the circumstances before reaching a judgment and reacting to situations of turmoil, tragedy, and trial.

Our Heavenly Father desires us to be patient and practice patience in our lives daily as patience is of the Heavenly Father and is a product of faith, hope, honesty, and good heartedness. Patience in our reactions to others is discussed in Luke 8:15. Oftentimes, our age is a determining factor of our patience; with advanced age comes wisdom, sound faith, and even temperament that increase our patience.

When our faith is tried our patience is being tested and growth becomes the result. With patience, we reach our desired outcome; hasty actions often bring on regret, poor decisions, and revenge-type situations. Patience is formulated in a person when they endure trying and turbulent times; we are urged to believe in the promises of God our Heavenly Father and react as such.

Matthew 18:26 encourages us to seek patience from our Heavenly Father on a regular basis in every action of our lives. Practice patience with changes we must endure that we do not wish to happen. Practice patience during the hard times in your life when things aren't going your way.

One of my personal favorite scriptures is Hebrews 12:1 the suggestion to run our own race and practice patience for obstacles in our lives that we cannot control. Have joyous faith that the Heavenly Father is in control, be patient and believe in His divine will for us and our lives. The will of the Heavenly Father is much better than what we could ever think or imagine. Patience of hope equals belief in better things to come. Without this is death and despair.

> Every word of God is pure: He is a shield unto
> them that put their trust in Him.
> —Proverbs 30:5

Practice patience daily, grow and mature in the Heavenly Father that He will strengthen you during the storms of life, lead your path, and teach you to be patient and trust in His direction. Do not allow another to steal your patience or suggest you be hasty in decision making and/or in actions that you take. This will steal your joy that is provided by our Heavenly Father and give someone else control of your state of mind and emotion.

Be respectful of the opinions of others, but as suggested, run your own race, remain calm in every situation and without turmoil and fear, and grow in your Heavenly Father. Personally, I practice if it isn't going to kill me, I don't worry about it. I don't do things to place myself in danger or act haphazardly or reckless, but I live daily without outside opinion, haters interfering and stealing my joy, and run my own race.

I am keenly aware as you should be too, not everyone wants you to succeed, have dreams larger than they can imagine, and wants to see you happy and prosper; do not allow these people to steal your patience, your joy, your happiness, or your peace.

Peace from our Heavenly Father is a gift. Grace and peace are what your Heavenly Father desires for you, happiness, cheerful spirit, and calm in calamity. The Bible states over and over grace and peace from God our Heavenly Father to all who believe and accept His great love.

The fruit of the spirit of God our Heavenly Father is love, joy, peace, longsuffering, gentleness, goodness, faith, meekness, and temperance as stated in Galatians 5:22–23. Christ is our peace, stay close to Him, call upon Him in trials and suffering for relief and protection. Christ our Heavenly Father is the peace of the past, the present, and the future.

Peace is calmness and contentment that we feel deep in our hearts, mind, and spirit. Peace allows us to remain consistent in trials, calm with misfortune, and certain with the unknown. Peace comes from our ever growing relationship with our Heavenly Father. Regardless of where you are in your walk with the Lord, remain at peace and know He is with you leading your path, lighting your way, and moving obstacles others may place in your path.

Be aware the devil comes in many forms, in many faces, and many deceiving attributes to disrupt what brings you joy. The devil in his hateful nasty spirit intends only harm to you! He and his army of tortured and mean spirits hate to see you happy; accept that as they are cunning, deceiving, and fear the Heavenly Father and His love and calm.

Evil only wishes to steal joy and calmness. You proceed with your life unscathed by his insulting, insensitive, and oftentimes childish actions. Hold your head up and remain calm regardless of what is going on around you and know you have the love and calm of the Heavenly Father and that evilness cannot touch you unless you allow it!

My computer completely froze writing this paragraph. I had to shut it off and turn in on again. Gracefully, auto-recovery saved my work that otherwise would have been lost; praise God for His grace to not allow this to happen. Devil took a nosedive straight back to where he came from because he was unable to ruin the work of the Heavenly Father and detour my mood. My mind and spirit are saying get a life devil mine is occupied with the Heavenly Father, Amen.

We are all children of the Heavenly Father regardless of the worshipping practice we have, He loves each of us the same. Every nation enjoys peace through Christ the Heavenly Father. Our Heavenly Father qualifies us all equally in His eyes and we all enjoy an abundance of His peace and love if we simply believe.

The Lord came to the earth He created to show us peace and help us to overcome the trials of the world. For those who believe He tells us in John 14:27 to not be bothered or afraid, find peace in God our Heavenly Father, peace that is not offered of the world. Our Heavenly Father overcame the trials of the world to show us peace and for those who believe He wants us to remain in peace and always be of good cheer as stated in John 16:33.

Peace offers us light in the darkness. Peace provides us calm in the fear of death and in times of trouble. Praise your Heavenly Father in all His glory, wisdom, and goodness for providing us such peace to count upon. Avoid conflict that drives us apart and causes strife. Live with the principles of acceptance, love, and joy.

Don't be afraid just believe.

—Mark 5:36

Resurrection can be a time of renewal of something that once was but went out of fashion, a revival situation, or a rebirth of an idea. Resurrection also describes rising from the dead as with Jesus Christ; after His death on the cross and three days in the tomb, He arose from the dead to go be with our Heavenly Father.

Acts 23:6 clearly states that everyone cannot conceive of such a notion and will not believe or understand, so we as believers in the Heavenly Father should expect this and be as simple in explanation as we possibly can when discussing the resurrection of Christ.

The resurrection of Jesus was the point of knowing He was the Son of God the Heavenly Father, the point which should strengthen our faith and belief in heaven and a life after death as preached and promised.

Jesus walked among us in our same flesh, in the same worldly environment, and then was put to death, as we will surely die. His resurrection was our promise and hope of life after death as believers. We as believers in the Heavenly Father will be treated the same and resurrected with the spirit and glory of the Heavenly Father to live a life in the heavens after death. A life free of sorrow, pain, affliction, and the fear of death.

If we die in belief and faith, we will rise in belief and faith to meet our Heavenly Father, the host of the heavens. We will once again see loved ones lost who believed, we will rejoice and praise the Heavenly Father for His glory and goodness that we see and enjoy. We die once and the faith we have in our Heavenly Father removes the fear of death and replaces it with hope of better things to come.

With resurrection and faith, death loses its control over you, no more temptation of sin or wrongdoings. There is power in your relationship with the Heavenly Father, power in the knowledge of His death and resurrection, and power in your belief of Christ as this determines your resurrection and removes fear from death and the unknown.

Resurrection and renewal come only from Christ. Receive the words and works of the Bible regarding our Heavenly Father and His resurrection. Be careful and cautious to not let the world steal your belief in the resurrection. It would be unwise to reform to the resurrection as a thing of the past and you are lost to resurrection and the Heavenly Father.

Doubters and nonbelievers as we discussed may not understand, don't have minds that can conceive, and lack heart and souls full of love and awareness of the Heavenly Father. Do not let anyone steal your faith as the Heavenly Father will never walk away from you, never cease loving you, and certainly never give up on you or His promises to you.

The Bible urges us to have faith in the resurrection of Christ. Proclaim life in resurrection as promised by our Heavenly Father and teach the resurrection to new believers. Resurrection is a source of hope and supports faith in the Heavenly Father.

The Heavenly Father allowed there to be witness to His death and resurrection to pass along the message and continue to teach and preach the resurrection to generations of believers to come. The Heavenly Father also allowed there to be death for Lazarus and witness to his resurrection even after four days of being bound in burial cloths and in a tomb: Lazarus's sister Martha telling Jesus he surely stink. Once our Heavenly Father spoke to Lazarus to rise and walk, he was whole again as if nothing had ever happened. This was witnessed to be testament to the resurrection power of our Heavenly Father.

Expect doubters of your faith, expect questions from nonbelievers, and backlash against you for your faith and belief in resurrection. Always revert to the Bible and understand not everyone can comprehend the resurrection of Christ. Know it is not uncommon as believes that we question our faith at times and need reassurance. Reassurance that is readily available in your Bible, in your talks with God the Heavenly Father, and reassurance in those who have gone before us believing and provided our foundation of faith.

I cannot stress this enough, do not allow another's ignorance of our Heavenly Father to steal your joy, harm your faith, or make you doubt yourself and your belief. Regardless of religion, denomination, or practices, our Heavenly Father remains the same. It is natural as years pass and generations change and are exposed to new ideas that things change some, but our Heavenly Father remains the constant in our lives.

> Jesus the light of the world came so we could find our way to God. Jesus the lamb of God, died upon the cross so we could receive the salvation of God. Jesus the bright and morning star, arose from the dead so we could live forever with God.
> —John 8:12

My prayer for you:

Heavenly Father, as we come before you once again, hear our prayers of peace, patience, and resurrection. Heavenly Father, offer us grace for those things that come against us meaning to harm us for our prayers and beliefs. Heavenly Father, provide strength and peace in trials, patience with understanding, and the hope of resurrection and better things to come. Heavenly Father, thank you that we can enjoy peace when the world around us is troubled, patience in our faith, and the hope of resurrection that allows us to live free from the fears of death, the past, and negativity.

Amen.

CHAPTER 18

God the Father

God the Father is friend, faith, and hope. Our Heavenly Father is always there if we just simply reach out and speak His name. A never-ending source of kindness, love, compassion, strength, and support that cannot be taken from us if we only believe. God the Heavenly Father is perfect, His ways are perfect, and He leads us with His perfection. The Heavenly Father is strength and protection for those who believe and trust Him.

Praise your Heavenly Father for His grace and glory in every situation in your life because He has equipped you to endure and be able to handle whatever comes either large or small. You are prepared and He is your backup if you simply reach out to Him. The salvation you have when you believe and trust in the Heavenly Father is your shield against evil, the turmoil of the world, and your own doubting thoughts.

Praise God and keep Him close in your heart and mind; He is the greatest source of strength you possess, the unrelenting ally in any situation, and the most overwhelming sense of peace and love you will ever possess.

God is gracious to forgive our mistakes if we just ask for that forgiveness then stop thinking of it, stop acting on it, and proceed with life looking and moving forward. Nehemiah 9:17 tells us God is without mistakes, gracious, forgiving, merciful, slow to anger, and offers us great tenderness if we will accept it. If you believe, you will hear God's words if you do not believe you cannot expect to hear the word of God, our Heavenly Father.

God is the creator of the universe. Humans are builders, architects, and artists working with what God has laid before them. For a microorganism to grow and develop, there must be perfect circumstances; God provided these perfect circumstances. There is no science that lays out the founding of the earth, the precise moment when conditions were right for one organism to spontaneously start to grow and develop into every organism that we know today.

There is no explanation why we are the miracle of humans and the human body. No science to prove why we are alone in the solar system. More importantly, there is no science to disprove the perfect timing of the sun and moon, the ebb and flow of the tides, the seasons of death and rebirth we see in our environment, the atmosphere in which we live and breathe, and the Heavenly Father or His time on earth.

Regardless of race, religion, denomination, practice, spirituality, and nationality, there is but one God/Heavenly Father and with the natural process of life and adapting to our surroundings (evolutionary processes) we have changed over the years, but the faith, love, strength, hope, and mercy of the Heavenly Father has remained the same. The perfection in the creation of the earth remains unequalled to anything we know today.

We each may interpret what we read, see, and feel differently and we all have our own special relationship with the Heavenly Father, and this is normal. Act your faith, don't just profess it. Let your actions speak to your faith, faith that has survived thousands of years, that cannot be eradicated, and that is enjoyed by the brightest minds the world has ever known. Revelation 21:5 tells us to write; write for the word of God our Heavenly Father is true, faithful, and everlasting. Our Heavenly Father is the Alpha and Omega, our beginning and our end.

My prayer for you:
Heavenly Father, thank you for Your never-ending love, strength, and protection. Heavenly Father, thank you for the wis-

dom to believe and trust You. Heavenly Father, thank you that we enjoy all the beauty the earth has to offer. Heavenly Father, allow the actions of Your children to speak volumes toward your goodness and lead nonbelievers to You. Heavenly Father, keep us engaged and active in our relationships with You, professing our commitment to You as our God.

Amen.

> Perhaps this is the moment for which you have
> been created.
>
> —Ester 4:14

Learn from these believers/scientists who are not in the Bible and are not preached about but have shaped the world and thoughts of the world as we know it today:

Louis Pasteur (disproved spontaneous growth from one organism)

Albert Einstein

The Apollo 11 mission astronauts

Galileo Galilei (Galileo)

Isaac Newton

Lord William Kelvin

Charles Darwin (never denied the existence of God)

Werner Heisenberg

Francis Collins (refuses to deny the existence of God)

REFERENCES

The Holy Bible, Original King James Version (1993) Mid America
    Bible Society, Gordonville, TN.

Saint Louis University School of Nursing (2004), Children of God;
    Saint Louis, MO.

William Newton Clark (unknown date) *The Joy Faith Brings*.

ABOUT THE AUTHOR

Patricia J. Vanderpool is a Doctor of Nursing Practice (DNP), entrepreneur, writer, professor, mother, daughter, friend, and the author of *A Love Affair with God*. She reads most anything she gets her hands on including labels before they became popular and has been told more than once that she spends a lot of time with her nose stuck in a book.

As a professionally trained nurse practitioner and educator, Patricia has spent the last thirty years listening too and caring for people. Her passion for reading and writing has allowed her to author several educational articles for professional publication, a novel titled *Absolutely Despicable* with Austin McCauley publishers, and this her second work.

Patricia has a Doctorate from Texas Christian University, a dual Master's from Saint Louis University, and a post-Master's from Saint Louis University. Patricia is certified to practice both adult and family practice as well as educate. Patricia enjoyed creative writing as part of her undergraduate work. Patricia has authored books, songs, teaching aides, and articles. She graduated in the top 15 percent of the graduating class at Texas Christian University and is a member of Golden Key Honor Society and in the top 5 percent of the nursing class and is a member of the Nursing Honor Society Sigma Theta Tau. Patricia is an entrepreneur and owns and operates a private healthcare practice. Patricia teaches as adjunct faculty at a Christ-centered institution. Patricia's works are highly anticipated as they are enlightening, entertaining, educational, and honest. This book by Patricia honors our Heavenly Father.

Indiana based Doctor, Nurse Practitioner, Educator, Author Patricia Vanderpool is known for practicing kindness as kindness is simple, life-altering, and priceless. Patricia is a dynamic individual enjoying everything life has to offer, always reaching for the sky knowing success and failure are both steppingstones down the path of life. Patricia can always be found standing up for what she believes, promoting her convictions, and supporting others.

CPSIA information can be obtained
at www.ICGtesting.com
Printed in the USA
BVHW092043290322
632749BV00004B/577